SO-AYA-026

CONTENTS

INTRODUCTION

T eresa Shook is a retired lawyer from Hawaii. She was very upset when Donald Trump was elected president. She knew others were, too. She wanted to show that many women rejected Trump's disrespectful attitudes toward women and minorities. On the evening of Election Day 2016, Shook wrote a Facebook post. She proposed a Women's March in Washington, DC. According to the *Washington Post*, she had ten thousand positive responses by the next morning. The numbers continued to grow. Shook was overwhelmed. She let veteran activists plan the march.

Planners wanted to make a strong statement against Donald Trump's presidency. They decided to hold the Women's March the day after his inauguration, January 21, 2017. Inauguration crowds were much smaller than usual. But the Women's March was huge. The *New York Times* reported that it was at least three times as large as the inauguration. The *Guardian* later placed the attendance at one million. Whole families—men, women, children, and grandparents—marched. The march was very peaceful. There were no arrests.

At the same time, "sister marches" occurred around the United States and the world. The *Guardian* reported 500,000 marchers in Los Angeles, 250,000 in Chicago, 200,000 in New York, 100,000 in Boston, and thousands in other cities. Those who could not

THE NEED TO KNOW

EVERYTHING YOU NEED TO KNOW ABOUT

SEXISM

CAROL HAND

Rosen
YA™
New York

Published in 2018 by The Rosen Publishing Group, Inc.
29 East 21st Street, New York, NY 10010

Library of Congress Cataloging-in-Publication Data

Names: Hand, Carol, 1945– author.
Title: Everything you need to know about sexism / Carol Hand.
Description: New York : Rosen Publishing, 2018 | Series: The need to know library | Audience: Grades 7–12. | Includes bibliographical references and index.
Identifiers: LCCN 2017022210| ISBN 9781508176800 (library bound) | ISBN 9781508176794 (pbk.) | ISBN 9781508176824 (6 pack) Subjects: LCSH: Sexism—Juvenile literature. | Sex discrimination against women—Juvenile literature. | Sex role—Juvenile literature. Classification: LCC HQ1237 .H36 2018 | DDC 305.3—dc23 LC record available at https://lccn.loc.gov/2017022210

Manufactured in the United States of America

Despite a million protesters in Washington, DC, the Women's March on January 21, 2017, was totally peaceful. No arrests were reported. The same was true in other cities.

travel staged marches in their hometowns. Americans abroad, with local supporters, formed huge crowds in London, Paris, Mexico City, Sydney, and other cities. *USA Today* reported that an estimated 2.6 million people participated in 673 marches in all fifty states and thirty-two countries. There was even a small march in Antarctica.

Many people marched against Trump. They protested his sexism by wearing pink knitted "pussy hats." They objected to his campaign promises to limit women's health and reproductive rights. They objected to his hate- and insult-ridden campaign. He had insulted many groups, including Hispanics, Muslims, blacks, war heroes, and disabled people.

Organizers and marchers had a positive, inclusive message. They marched for people of all genders, all colors, the LGBTQ+ community, and immigrants and refugees. Their goal, described in Vox, was "to affirm our shared humanity and pronounce our bold message of resistance and self-determination." They rallied around the statement by Hillary Clinton (whom Trump defeated) that "women's rights are human rights." They wanted to emphasize that all people should control their own bodies.

On Facebook, a woman named Christy said the march was unnecessary. If Americans don't have everything they need, she said, it's their own fault. Marching would not change that. Many followers agreed with her. Communication strategist Susan Speer answered Christy's comments. Speer said, "I didn't march because I personally feel marginalized. I marched because I can. I marched because a lot of women can't, even if you don't see them." Speer marched for women facing prejudice because they have same-sex partners. She marched for women who have minimum wage jobs, lack access to health care, and have no way to get an education. Speer and other marchers stood up for these people in need.

What did the march accomplish? "I think it will be remembered as the biggest march on Washington ever," said march founder Theresa Shook. "I am hearing from a lot of people that it … woke up their activism and their love of their country. A lot of women said they had been quiet, and they won't be quiet anymore."

CHAPTER ONE

DOES SEXISM REALLY EXIST?

D onald Trump's election became a rallying cry for women around the country. Trump's language was demeaning toward women. On a video made public during his campaign, he bragged that his fame helped him take sexual advantage of women. When interviewed by Anderson Cooper of CNN, he said, "It's just words" and just "locker room talk." Trump often bases his opinions of women only on their looks. Reporter Claire Cohen listed terms he has used to describe women. These included "fat," "pig," "dog," "slob," and "disgusting animal."

Trump says he has no time for political correctness. This is avoiding words and phrases that offend or hurt certain people or groups. The rules of political correctness may change as the culture changes. But avoiding such words or expressions often just requires courtesy and respect. Women have fought back against Trump's sexist words and actions. They began with the Women's March. They planned ways to make their voices heard during the Trump administration. Many have never before been political. But they are running for political

Donald Trump is well-known for saying whatever he thinks. His judgments of women based on their appearance are a form of sexism.

office. They are tired of sexism, and they plan to do something about it.

What exactly is sexism? Does it really exist? Does it matter what words are used to describe women? Evidence shows that sexism is very real. Sexist attitudes toward women carry over into all aspects of their lives.

SOME DEFINITIONS

Sexism occurs when women are treated unfairly and differently from men. It is a form of prejudice or discrimination. People who show prejudice are biased against a group, such as women. Their opinion about the group is not based on facts or evidence. They show disrespect, intolerance, or hatred. Prejudice is a feeling or attitude, rather than an action. Discrimination involves action. It is unfair or biased treatment of a group of people. Prejudice and discrimination cause harm to the group or to individuals.

Feminists are people who believe women and men should have equal rights and opportunities. Feminists can be individuals of any gender. Most feminists include power in their definition of sexism. They point out that, throughout history, men have had power and

SEX VS. GENDER

The terms "sex" and "gender" are not quite the same. "Sex" refers to biological differences. This includes differences in sex organs and genetics, or sex chromosomes. Females have two X chromosomes; males have an X and a Y. A few people are born with other patterns of sex chromosomes, such as XO, XXY, or XXX. Genes do not change. According to Tim Newman, in *Medical News Today*, about one in 1,500 babies are intersex. They have both male and female genitals.

"Gender" refers to the social and cultural role of each sex within a society. Gender roles vary in different societies. Children learn how each gender is expected to behave. They are taught by adults, peers, and media. For example, women are often expected to do child care, and men are expected to earn money. But these roles can change. Women and men in many societies are becoming more equal. Gender identity is how each person sees himself or herself. Sometimes a person's internal feeling does not match the gender they were assigned at birth. These people are called transgender, or trans. Transgender people can also be victims of sexism as well as homophobia and transphobia.

privilege. Women have had less power, or none at all. Therefore, feminists define sexism as prejudice plus power. They say sexism occurs when men exert unfair power over women. They do not accept the idea that women can be sexist toward men because men already hold the power.

Sociologists (experts in the study of human society) recognize two types of sexism. Hostile sexism involves angry, negative attitudes toward women. These sexists treat women badly. They may bully women, refuse them equal treatment, or sexually harass them. The other type is benevolent sexism. "Benevolent" means good or kind. In this type of sexism, women are considered weak, or like "delicate flowers." Benevolent sexists think women need protection and special treatment. They may, therefore, bar women from certain jobs. Both types of sexism use stereotypes of women. They see women as inferior and less capable than men. They consider women unequal to men and less deserving of respect.

CHANGING TREATMENT OF WOMEN

Treatment of women has improved dramatically since the United States was founded. Women can vote and own property. They can hold office and have careers. Laws protect them from discrimination and abuse. Legally, women are now mostly equal to men. But they still face social and cultural discrimination. They face unequal pay or job opportunities. Many fields, such as engineering and computer science, are still male dominated. Only a

Women in today's world are excelling in business, science, and other areas. Here, a young businesswoman takes the lead, explaining strategy in a meeting.

small percentage of elected officials are women. Women are often judged on appearance instead of abilities. They experience sexual harassment and bullying.

Ray Jablonski, in Cleveland.com, reported on the findings of a 2015 United Nations delegation of human rights experts. They identified five areas in which US women have fewer rights or are less well treated than women in other developed countries. The areas include pay, maternity leave, affordable child care, reproductive rights, and violence against women. Dina Leygerman, in Medium, says women in New Zealand earn 5.6 percent less than men for the same work. American women

In 2011, President Barack Obama awarded the National Medal of Technology to Yvonne C. Brill. Her innovations in rocket propulsion technology for communication satellites were groundbreaking.

earn 20 percent less. The pay gap is even greater for women of color. In Iceland, 44 percent of chief executive officers, CEOs, are women. In the United States, only 4 percent are women. According to the World Economic Forum, the United States ranks twenty-eighth in the world in women's equality. It ranks below Rwanda, the Philippines, and Nicaragua, among others.

SEXISM THROUGHOUT LIFE

Sexism can occur anytime during a woman's life, from birth through old age. Sometimes it even occurs after death. Rocket scientist Yvonne Brill died in 2013 at age eighty-eight. Her death notice was in the *New York Times*. The first paragraph described her as a great cook who followed her husband from job to job and took eight years off to raise three children. Her son called her "the world's best mom." Only in the second paragraph did the *New York Times* mention that she also "invented a propulsion system to help keep communications satellites from slipping out of their orbits." Readers pointed out that the article would have been different for a male scientist (Albert Einstein, for example). Parenting and cooking skills would not have been mentioned. William McDonald, the column's editor, saw nothing wrong with the article. He said it never occurred to him that it would be considered sexist.

Sexism definitely still exists. It limits women's opportunities. It often prevents full development of their abilities. It makes all aspects of their lives more difficult.

MYTHS AND FACTS

MYTH: All feminists are radical women who hate men.

FACT: Feminists can be any gender. They believe men and women should have equal rights and opportunities.

MYTH: Sexism no longer exists; therefore, feminism is no longer needed.

FACT: Women have more rights than in the past. However, they are still treated unequally. Sexism still exists throughout society, in homes, schools, and workplaces.

MYTH: Feminism seeks to free women at the expense of men.

FACT: Society sets boundaries for both men and women. Feminists want both men and women to be free to be themselves. For example, women should be free to be strong leaders. Men should be free to show emotion.

CHAPTER TWO

GROWING UP IN A SEXIST WORLD

S exism begins with dressing female babies in pink and male babies in blue. Colors separate the sexes. They help children fit into society's male-female roles. A century ago, the colors were opposite. Smithsonian quotes a 1918 article from a children's clothing company: "The generally accepted rule is pink for the boys, and blue for the girls. The reason is that pink, being a more decided and stronger color, is more suitable for the boy, while blue, which is more delicate and dainty, is prettier for the girl." The colors have switched, but the attitude remains the same: boys are strong; girls are dainty and delicate.

ATTITUDES AND EXPECTATIONS

Adults teach gender stereotypes early. A three-year-old girl picked up a stethoscope in a toy store. A nearby stranger asked, "Are you going to be a nurse?" Reporter Laura Bates of the *Guardian* asks, would a boy have been asked the same thing? People compliment little

Many children learn early that pink is for girls, while blue is for boys. These gender-based stereotypes carry over into behavioral expectations for boys and girls.

girls for being pretty and polite. They tell little boys how "big and strong" they are. Bates notes that it is fine for boys or girls to choose these roles, but often they are not given a choice. Many young girls begin to think they cannot play football or be doctors or lawyers, simply because they are girls.

Child development experts Olaiya E. Aina and Petronella A. Cameron state that stereotypes are well developed by age five. Princes in Disney movies are admired for their bravery and actions, princesses for their beauty or singing. These movies strongly influence children. Books also influence gender roles.

Aina and Cameron describe a study of award-winning children's books. In these books, male main characters outnumbered females three to one. Twenty-one of twenty-five books showed pictures of women wearing aprons. If children cannot identify with characters in books and movies, they feel less important and less capable.

Gender stereotyping affects everything from play to career choice. In separate preschool play groups, girls choose more family or housekeeping roles. Boys choose action-adventure play. But if play areas are gender neutral, boys and girls play together, with the same toys. When given a choice of careers, both boys and girls reject traditional female roles. They learn early that these roles are less valued than male roles. If these stereotypes are not corrected, Aina and Cameron say, girls will have lower self-esteem and lower school performance.

THE CLOTHING WARS

Parents can now learn the sex of their unborn children. They decorate nurseries and buy clothes based on the baby's gender. Even diapers are sometimes color coded by gender. Advertisers use this to sell more. The trend continues with older children. Laura Willard, in a 2015 article on Upworthy, cited examples of sexist clothing. A onesie for baby boys said, "I'm super." The same style for baby girls said, "I hate my thighs." In 2013, a girls' T-shirt sold by the store Children's Place gave a list of "My best subjects." Choices for shopping, music, and dancing were checked. "Math" was unchecked. Under "Math," it said "Well, Nobody's Perfect." Mothers fought back. They had intelligent, capable daughters. They wanted girls' clothes to reflect this. They started businesses to produce clothes that do reflect intelligence.

Willard describes the movement, #ClothesWithoutLimits, formed by ten mothers. Their clothes are designed to empower girls and express all their interests. One T-shirt says "Smart Girls Club." Another has a picture of a T. rex and the slogan "Half of all T. rexes were girls!" A pink T-shirt says, "Forget Princess, Call Me President." The new clothing move-

As these pink and blue cupcakes for a baby shower show, gender stereotyping starts even before the baby is born.

ment empowers both women and girls. One company, buddingSTEM, produces science-themed clothes for girls. Willard quotes its co-founder Jennifer Muhm: "This is an amazing group of like-minded women who care deeply about breaking down the gender stereotypes in girls' clothing today."

BOYS' AND GIRLS' TOYS

Toys show clearly how differently people treat boys and girls. Boys' toys stress action, leadership, science, and technology. They highlight jobs that have power

A young girl looks at a doll based on the Disney film *The Princess and the Frog*. Companies such as Disney aggressively market gender-biased toys to children.

and prestige—for example, soldiers, doctors, and engineers. Girls' toys concentrate on cooking and housekeeping, beauty and fashion, and, of course, child care. At the Boys' Toys page on toysrus.com, the top categories are Action Figures, Video Games, and Building Sets. The Girls' Toys page focuses on Dolls, Arts & Crafts, and Bath, Beauty & Accessories. The girls' Pretend Play category includes a play microwave, vacuum cleaner, and Disney-themed Cosmetic Castle.

But do children want these differences, or is this simply the message they receive? It is definitely the message, according to Nancy Kaffer, writing in the Daily Beast. Kaffer says, "Any parent of small children can tell you gender-based toys are stupid—boys like dolls, and girls like trucks, at least until we teach them they shouldn't." She is backed up by the National Association for the Education of Young Children. This group says limiting toys based on gender is not good for children. The best educational toys are either neutral or moderately masculine. To develop necessary skills, girls must play with these toys.

WHEN GIRLS ARE TREATED EQUALLY

When Roma Agrawal was eight years old, she and her sister received a playhouse for their Barbie dolls. It was not assembled. The girls excitedly used their Meccano set to assemble the playhouse. They built two cranes and a digger. They pretended their dolls were operating the machinery and building their new home. Agrawal's parents made sure the sisters had all kinds of toys and

GIRLS AND BOYS ON THE SAME TEAM?

Some girls want to play sports that are typically reserved for boys, such as football. According to shape.com, 1,600 girls played on football teams with boys in US high schools in 2015. Riley Fox played for R. L. Paschal High School in Fort Worth, Texas. Her coach said she was one of the best kickers he had ever seen. Erin DiMeglio was the first female quarterback in south Florida high school football history. In her first game in 2012, DiMeglio made a pass that won the game.

Some people do not approve of coed teams. People fear girls may get hurt because boys tend to be larger and stronger. Boys may fear failing in front of girls. Girls may be more timid and not perform at their best if boys are present. Boys and girls may need different styles of uniforms and separate locker rooms. These things may make running the team more difficult.

Child psychologist Laura E. Berk (quoted by Leigh Reason on Livestrong.com) likes coed sports. She thinks the best way to prevent gender stereotyping is to involve kids in coed sports early. They should be separated by ability and mental development, not gender. Boys and girls on a team together develop strong friendships. They develop social skills and have fun. Berk says girls involved in coed sports get better grades. They have better body images and higher self-esteem.

experiences. They had Barbie dolls and took dance lessons. They also had building toys and played cops and robbers. They grew up thinking they could do anything. Agrawal became a structural engineer. She helped build the Shard, western Europe's tallest building.

But, Agrawal says, most girls do not have the choices she had. They are given only "mirrors and hairbrushes, cooking sets, and dolls (all in pink)." They are taught that girls should value appearance and nurturing. Boys are given "science toys, building blocks, and toys for play-fighting." They are taught to value experimentation and confrontation. Parents and teachers often tell older girls that science and engineering are not for them. Girls think they cannot succeed, so they do not try.

For girls to be equal in society, they need equal opportunities. They need to be considered capable by parents and teachers and in books and media. They need to be considered equal to boys.

CHAPTER THREE

GETTING EDUCATED IN A SEXIST WORLD

A merican girls, like boys, have the right to an education. But sexism is still an issue in schools. Boys and girls are treated differently and achieve differently. They may have access to different programs and opportunities. This is particularly true in STEM (science, technology, engineering, and math) areas. Girls may even suffer sexual harassment in schools.

GENDER BIAS IN TEACHING

Sexism in education can begin as early as preschool, according to child development experts Olaiya Aina and Petronella A. Cameron. Many preschool books and classroom materials are gender biased. Teachers can promote gender bias by responding differently to boys and girls. They may be unaware of this. A study showed that boys called out in class eight times more often than girls. Their comments were often off topic, yet teachers always responded. But when girls called out, the teacher was more likely to reminded her not to

Girls can, and should, begin to learn science and use science equipment early in their school careers. This makes them more confident of their own abilities.

talk until called upon. If this pattern continues through-out twelve years of school, girls can suffer serious self-esteem issues. Aina and Cameron suggest ways to limit gender stereotyping. Teachers can replace gender-biased materials with gender-neutral ones. They can encourage cross-gender activities and play centers. They can read books that provide positive role models for all sexes.

Gender bias can continue throughout school. Home-work is a good example. Laura Bates, in the *Guardian*, shared examples of sexist homework assignments for older students. One teacher asked kids to research an inventor. She gave a list of questions to answer, starting with, "Who was he?" Another assignment directed students to use a specific website for research. The site listed twenty-one historical people, but only two were women. Writing students were asked to compare the qualities of a "good wife" in biblical times versus modern times. There was no comparable assignment comparing "good husbands." Physics students used pictures of men shooting arrows, climbing trees, and lifting weights. The only woman shown was pushing a baby stroller.

GENDER BIAS IN STEM

People, including many children, assume girls are less able than boys to succeed in STEM careers. In 2014, Campbell Leaper and Christia Spears Brown did a study on sexism in STEM. They showed that girls in primary and middle school perform the same as boys on math tests. But in high school and college, girls become less interested in math. They perform slightly less well on math tests. Boys score much better on tests in physics, engineering, and computer science. There are fewer women with careers in these fields. The National Center for Education Statistics (NCES) said women received 57 percent of bachelor's degrees in 2013. But they received only 43 percent of mathematics degrees. Percentages of women graduating with degrees in other STEM fields were even smaller: 20 percent of degrees in physics, 18 percent in engineering, and 16 percent in physics.

Gender bias is one of several factors causing girls and women to achieve less well in STEM fields. Gender bias affects girls' self-esteem. If a girl thinks, "I'm not good enough. I can't do math (or science)," her test scores suffer. Teens hear negative comments about girls' math and science abilities from peers, teachers, coaches, and parents. Professors Lee Shumow and Jennifer A. Schmidt, in the Huffington Post, say teachers are strongly biased in favor of boys. Both male and female teachers spend 40 percent more time helping boys in science classes. Teachers consider boys who do well in science to be talented. They see girls as hard workers.

But fields such as reading, literature, and the arts are stereotyped as "feminine." Girls are expected to do well in them, and boys less well. Boys who excel in these areas are often teased by male peers. Boys from lower-income families or ethnic minorities especially are often pressured to be tough and masculine. They often then do poorly or do not seek help in these subjects.

GENDER BIAS IN SPORTS

Girls have traditionally been shortchanged in school sports. Passage of the 1972 Title IX of the Civil Rights Act meant girls could no longer be barred from school sports (or other educational programs) that received government funds. In 1972, only 4 percent of girls participated in high school sports. By 2009, 40 per-

Female high school wrestlers defy gender stereotypes. Rosemary Flores and Sarah Andresen, both of New York City, compete in a youth wrestling exhibition during the 2013 Beat the Streets Gala.

cent of girls participated. The percentage of boys (50 percent) remained unchanged.

Title IX has not removed sexism from sports. Certain sports, such as football and wrestling, are still seen as boys' sports. Cheerleading and ballet are seen as activities for girls. As girls get older, they are often pressured to drop out of sports. Boys might make negative comments about girls who play sports. Sometimes, other girls, teachers, and parents also discourage girls from playing sports. Many parents tend to support and encourage their sons more than their daughters.

SEXUAL HARASSMENT IN SCHOOLS

The American Association for University Women (AAUW) surveyed sexual harassment in grades seven to twelve. By grade twelve, 62 percent of girls and 32 percent of boys reported being sexually harassed, either in person or online. Harassment was related to the person's sexual attractiveness, weight, athletic ability, or gender characteristics. Those most likely to be harassed were LGBTQ+ youth and lower-income students.

Sexual harassment is common even in middle schools. A 2014 study reported in *US News & World Report* stated that one in four students from four midwestern middle schools reported harassment. This included unwanted sexual comments, touching, spreading rumors, and homophobic name-calling. School staff members often dismissed the behaviors. They said girls invited the harassment because of their dress or behavior. In the AAUW study, only 9 percent of those harassed reported the incident to a school staff member, and only about one-fourth mentioned it to parents, siblings, or friends. More girls than boys reported problems due to sexual harassment. Problems included trouble sleeping, depression, and anxiety. Girls missed school more often, their grades suffered, and some dropped out of activities.

REDUCING SEXISM IN SCHOOLS

Many girls do not recognize sexism by their teachers or coaches. They blame themselves for these prob-

SEXISM AND DRESS CODES

School dress codes often apply to girls, but seldom to boys. In hot weather, girls might like to wear shorts, short skirts, and tank tops. Sometimes they wear spaghetti straps or low-cut tops or show bare midriffs. Girls might say these clothes are cool and practical. But many school administrators say they are provocative and distracting. According to an article in *The Week*, boys' dress codes warn against "drinking, drug use, gangs, violence, or racism." Girls' dress codes simply say, "Don't be sexy." Emily, a California high school girl, says it is acceptable for boys in track to run shirtless on a hot day. But if a girl wears a bright-colored sports bra that shows through her white shirt, she is asked to change her clothes.

Mashable reported that girls at Montclair High School in New Jersey were "made to stand up in the middle of class to check the length of their shorts." At another school, a girl was given deten-

Kylee Opper models her chosen prom dress, which was deemed inappropriate, per the dress code adopted by her school.

(continued on the next page)

(continued from the previous page)

tion for wearing a halter-top dress because it exposed her shoulders. "Instead of teaching girls to cover up," Emily says, "we should be teaching everyone to stop sexualizing every aspect of a girl's body."

Girls (and parents) are starting to fight back against sexism in school dress codes. They are confronting administrators, doing in-school protests, and writing letters. Many are starting online petitions. Some schools are beginning to rethink their dress codes.

lems. But students can learn to recognize sexism. For example, when they see the lack of female US presidents, they can learn that this is due to sexism. It is not because women are poor leaders. They can apply this understanding to their own lives.

Avoiding or ignoring sexism does not relieve the stress it causes. Girls might respond to sexism by confronting the sexist person. They might discuss the situation with someone. Students in the AAUW study suggested allowing students to report problems anonymously. They requested an assigned person to talk to, online resources, and in-class discussions. They also wanted better enforcement of existing sexual-harassment policies. Having support from adults is also extremely important. But learning to recognize sexism is the first step to confronting it.

CHAPTER FOUR

SEXISM IN THE WORKPLACE

Sexism does not go away when a girl grows up and enters the workforce. Her ideas and contributions may be ignored or undervalued. She may be paid less and promoted less often than men. She may receive unwanted sexual advances. Things are much better than in the past—we no longer live in the days of *Mad Men*. But female workers are still treated differently from men.

THE WAGE GAP

As of 2010, 58.6 percent of American women were working or looking for work. This was 47 percent of the total workforce, according to the US Department of Labor. But there are several differences in the work lives of women and men.

One difference is the wage gap. Overall, says Jillian Berman in the Huffington Post, women make only seventy-seven cents for every dollar made by men. Recent female college graduates do slightly better.

Rutgers University graduates cheer President Barack Obama as he speaks at their 2016 commencement. Young women in this class will likely be paid better than those in previous generations.

Molly Redden, writing for the *Guardian*, says the wage gap is much greater for women of color. "For every dollar a white man is paid, white women are paid 81 cents, black women 65 cents, and Hispanic women 58 cents," Redden says. This means women earn an average of $7,600 to $10,000 less per year than men. This occurs in spite of the passage of the 2009 Lilly Ledbetter Fair Pay Act. This act makes pay discrimination on the basis of gender illegal.

Some pay differences are based on career choice. According to the International Labour Organization,

THE QUEEN OF CARBON

Dr. Mildred (Millie) Dresselhaus died on February 20, 2017, at age eighty-six. She had just appeared in a General Electric television commercial. GE was advertising its commitment to hiring more women. In the commercial, little girls play with Millie Dresselhaus dolls. Journalists wait for the next Dresselhaus sighting. The narrator asks, "What if we treated great female scientists like they were stars?"

Most people have probably never heard of Millie Dresselhaus. But she was a star in the scientific world. She was called the queen of carbon. She figured out how to use the element carbon in new materials and in nanotechnology (the science of extremely tiny particles). She developed the nanotube—a single-layer carbon sheet rolled into a hollow tube. Nanotubes are extremely strong, but only one ten-thousandth as wide as a human hair.

Dresselhaus came to the Massachusetts Institute of Technology (MIT) in 1960. Dresselhaus was one of two women on a scientific staff

Professor Mildred Dresselhaus won many honors, including the National Medal of Science and dozens of honorary doctorates.

(continued on the next page)

(*continued from the previous page*)

of 1,000 people. "We were pretty much invisible," she said. In 1968, she became the first woman promoted to full professor at MIT. In 1971, with a colleague, she organized MIT's first Woman's Forum to explore the roles of women in science. Dresselhaus worked throughout her career to make women scientists more visible. By 2017, MIT's faculty was 22 percent female.

most teachers, nurses, and social workers are women. Women have 60 percent of minimum-wage jobs and two-thirds of part-time jobs. These are all low-paying jobs. Far fewer women have high-paying professional, scientific, and technical careers.

Berman cites factors other than job choice that affect women's paychecks. Some employers think women need less money than men because men should make the family's living. Some think women will be poor employees because they will put their children first. Some think certain jobs are "men's work." These reasons are based on stereotypes about women. Also, about half of workers are not allowed to discuss salaries with their coworkers. Thus, women have no way to compare their salaries with those of men in their workplace. Women also have to work harder to advance. According to *Fortune* magazine, in 2016, only twenty-one of the top five hundred US companies (4.2 percent) had female CEOs. More than one-third of all major companies had no women in senior positions.

SUBTLE SEXISM

Men and women enter the workforce in about equal numbers. But as workers advance, percentages in upper management become increasingly male. Nathan Bomey, in *USA Today*, says men are 30 percent more likely than women to be promoted to manager. Why? Women are more likely to be ignored in meetings. They are given fewer challenging assignments. They are assigned smaller budgets and smaller staffs. They are often not consulted on important decisions.

Kathleen Elkins of Business Insider says women are often expected to do low-value "office housework." They are asked to answer phones, set up meetings, take notes, and get coffee. Men are not. If women refuse thankless jobs, they are considered selfish and not team players. These things are often not recognized as sexism, but they demean women and limit their performance. Eventually, many women quit because of long hours and frustration.

Tom Schuller, author of *The Paula Principle*, concludes that women typically work (and are paid) below their level of competence. Their education and abilities are undervalued and their talent is wasted.

SEXUAL HARASSMENT

Sexual harassment covers a wide variety of behaviors. One form is a workplace environment that tolerates sexist jokes and comments. Men often consider these comments harmless, but they embarrass or degrade women. Consistent sexist comments cause stress and create a hostile work environment. Less obvious behaviors include constant staring or repeatedly asking for dates. Jillian Berman reports in the Huffington Post that 83 percent of sexual harassment charges in 2010 were made by women.

Common types of harassment include leers, gestures, and pornographic texts. More physical types include unwanted touching, groping, or sexual assault. A survey by Michelle Ruiz in *Cosmopolitan* reported that one in three women ages eighteen to thirty-four has been sexually harassed at work. Women are targeted most often by male coworkers. Other harassers include customers or clients, male managers, and even female managers.

The study also discovered that 70 percent of women did not report harassment. Unless it involves rape or assault, harassment is not a crime. Although a woman could file a civil suit, reporting harassment is complicated. Often the harasser is careful to do nothing in public. This makes harassment a "he said, she said" situation. Also, the harasser may retaliate if reported. Many women often leave their jobs rather than report harassment. Sometimes, women do sue their employers. Many cases are settled out of court to avoid bad publicity for the employer. Only a few go to court and succeed.

OVERCOMING WORKPLACE SEXISM

Most companies have policies to prevent sexual harassment. These policies cover obvious forms of sexism. They are less effective in combating subtle types, such as sexist comments or expecting women to do office housekeeping. This means women must learn to recognize and combat sexism themselves. One way to fight sexism is to stay cool, but speak up. Maintaining a sense of humor can often get the point across. Lara Rutherford-Morrison, writing for Bustle, suggests statements such as: "Would you have said

In 2016, UCLA students protested the handling of a sexual misconduct case involving a professor and a graduate student. They demanded tougher administrative action against the professor.

that if I were a guy?" Or "I know I make great coffee, but is there some reason my coworkers never get asked to do it?" Sometimes telling a man his words or actions were inappropriate is enough.

If harassers do not respond to requests to stop, stronger measures are needed. Women should always be familiar with their company's sexual harassment policy. Keeping a log describing every incident provides evidence for a harassment claim. Going to a higher-up in the organization can help. A woman should know that filing a complaint means she will also be investigated. After the complaint is settled, she might still have to work with the harasser.

Sexism in the workplace will no doubt continue to exist. But the greatest cause for optimism is women themselves. They recognize sexist behavior and are willing to do something about it. Hana Schank and Elizabeth Wallace, reporting on a study of sexism for *The Atlantic*, summed it up: "…what we found interesting was the degree to which this generation of women felt newly empowered to stand up and shout about it."

CHAPTER FIVE

SEXISM IN THE HOME AND FAMILY

Most girls and young women assume they are equal to men. They expect careers equal to those of men. They recognize that sexism exists and are ready to challenge it at school and work. But can they overcome sexist attitudes within their own homes and families?

ARE THE 1950S REALLY OVER?

The typical 1950s attitude was "a woman's place is in the home." No matter how much today's young women value equality, many still struggle with this sexist attitude, left over from previous generations. These attitudes are instilled from childhood by parents and other family members.

British journalist Laura Bates documented examples of family-based sexism in her Everyday Sexism Project. A twelve-year-old girl was told by a female relative, "Men only marry women who can cook and clean. If they are educated, it's a bonus." A fourteen-year-

During the 1950s, women were primarily responsible for homemaking and child-care duties.

old's father ordered her to lose weight because no man wants to be seen with a "chubby wife." A twelve-year-old was in the kitchen. Her father's friend came in and said it was "nice to see a woman where she belongs." Another twelve-year-old was sexually assaulted. Her grandfather said she shouldn't have been wearing a skirt. She was wearing her school uniform. Bates calls such attitudes "institutional sexism." They are part of society and passed down through families. No one considers the damage they do to girls and women.

Fathers often practice a form of benevolent sexism. A father may give a grown daughter more money than he would give a son. He sees this as helping her, but he is implying she cannot take care of herself. He makes her more dependent. Or a father may feel that women have a "proper" role in society. He gives his daughter approval only when she fits that role. If she dresses or acts in a way he considers unfeminine, he shows his disapproval. This subtly makes her less free. She develops "gendered habits" that may restrict her growth as a person.

PRESSURE TO HAVE KIDS

Therapist Dr. Ellen Walker counseled a young woman who had mentioned to her mother and grandmother that she didn't want children. Their response was, "You *will* have children. You *must* have children." Not every response is so emphatic. But young women do feel pressure—sometimes constant pressure—from relatives to have children.

A national survey from the University of Nebraska shows that, in the 2010s, about 20 percent of US women remain child free. Some are childless by choice, others due to infertility or other reasons. Women who are childless by choice face more pressure to have kids but are less bothered by it. They do not think having children is necessary to be fulfilled as women. Only women who consider motherhood important to fulfillment are upset by not having children.

Columnist Margo Lockhart notes that women are programmed to want children and feel guilty for considering life without them. They do not discuss or even accept mixed feelings about motherhood. They do not want their children to feel unwanted. But, she says, "Giving our daughters permission not to be mothers does not devalue their lives… It gives women a broader sense of what they can become and do outside of motherhood."

BALANCING WORK AND FAMILY

Husbands are finally starting to take part in caring for home and family. But even in young families where both parents work, women are still mostly responsible for housework. According to a survey conducted by LeanIn.org and McKinsey & Co., 41 percent of women say they do more child care and 30 percent do more housework than their husbands. The study, reported in the *Wall Street Journal*, also showed that women

IS HOME TECHNOLOGY SEXIST?

After World War II, advertisers presented women with hundreds of new labor-saving household appliances. Home management and child care were just as empowering as working outside the home, they said. This attitude continues today, as advertisers push smart-home technology. According to an article in *Pacific Standard*, "... the best housewife is the one who knows enough to trust a smart-home system with her family's well-being." In its first round of ads, Google's smart-home technology package, Nest, featured "a grandpa, a toddler, a dad, and a dog." The off-screen mother was charged with setting up the system and keeping it functional. In other words, the woman is still the homemaker. Her primary job is taking care of her family.

Marketing shiny new household technology only to women assumes only women are responsible for home-making. It also sets them up to fail. With all this new technology, how can they not run a perfect home, have perfect children, and still have a fulfilling career outside the home? These ads do not tackle the unequal division of labor in the home, says sociologist Dr. Judy Wacjman. Like appliance ads of the 1950s, they offer a technological fix for a social problem.

In the 1950s, advertisers assured women they could be "queen of the home" with new appliances. In the 2010s, the technology has changed, but the message has not.

are five times more likely than men to stay home with children. Women who take time off work advance more slowly. But, because the husband's salary is usually higher, it makes economic sense for the woman to stay home. Psychologist and professor Stevan Hobfoll concludes, "The bottom line is that what men do is more valued—and men are still largely in charge."

Besides the pay inequality, Hobfoll says, there are other reasons that homemaking remains largely feminine. Society, including media, still assumes women are the homemakers. And, mothers may simply choose to spend more time with their children than fathers do. Also, money isn't everything. Career women who spend more time with their children report a higher quality of life than their husbands, who work longer hours.

Each family divides chores in the way that works best for them. Two-career couples work best when they plan and negotiate. There are always trade-offs: if the mother has a business trip, can the father take over home and child care responsibilities? If one partner is offered a great job across the country, is the other willing to leave his or her job and start over? To navigate these decisions, couples must talk. They must cooperate, rather than compete. They must work toward common goals.

HOUSEHUSBANDS AND WAHPS

The new generation is making new rules to balance home and family. This includes switching traditional gender roles. One example is the househusband. Some women have good-paying, fulfilling jobs or simply like working outside the home. Their husbands prefer to stay home, do the housework, and care for the kids. This traditional gender role reversal is gaining ground among men. A 2015 survey from Boston College found that 51 percent of millennial men were willing to be a stay-at-home parent (SAHP) if their wives made enough money. If women are comfortable taking on traditional male roles, the opposite should also be true, they say.

Another new trend is the work-at-home-parent (WAHP). Either or both parents may choose to work from home. Stu Gray and his wife are both WAHPs.

Being a work-at-home parent allows both mothers and fathers to combine work with family and child care. It decreases stress, and enables parents to have more time with their kids.

Gray points out many advantages over the nine-to-five job. Both parents have flexible schedules. They work fewer hours, taking projects only when they need or want them. They have more time to be with their small son. They work as a team, and they both love their chosen lifestyle.

Finally, in this new generation, many feminists are rethinking their past bias against women who choose to be housewives. Nikita Redcar, writing for Everyday Feminism, stresses that feminism should be inclusive. It should allow for women—and men—to make the decisions that work best for them. Women should have freedom of choice. Sometimes, this means choosing to remain home and be a housewife. And these women can still be feminists.

CHAPTER SIX

SEXISM IN POLITICS AND THE WIDER WORLD

In October 2016, Peter Beinart wrote in *The Atlantic* about Hillary Clinton's candidacy for president. He pointed out that Clinton was a very conventional presidential candidate—except for gender. Yet she received the highest unfavorable rating of any candidate since the question was first asked in 1980. White men saw her most unfavorably. The hostility against Clinton was too intense to be explained by her policies or her perceived flaws as a candidate. It was, Beinart concluded, a result of pure misogyny. It was hatred, contempt, and deep-seated prejudice against Clinton because she was a woman.

ROLE MODELS, POLITICS, AND SEXISM

Among many people, the political rise of Barack Obama and Hillary Clinton were hailed as evidence that both racism and sexism were declining in the United States. Yet Obama's election led to a rise in vicious racist talk. Clinton's candidacy led to an explosion of

While Hillary Clinton became a role model for millions of girls and young women during the 2016 presidential campaign, she was also the target of incredible misogyny.

misogyny. The latter showed up in pins and T-shirts worn by Trump supporters. They said things like "Trump that b*tch!" and "Life's a b*tch. Don't vote for one." Far-right political sites even portrayed Clinton as a devil. Trump encouraged this misogyny with belittling statements about Clinton and women in general.

Beinart cites research in social psychology to explain misogynistic attitudes. The idea of "precarious manhood" says that manhood must be earned and can be lost. Men greatly fear a loss of manhood, or emasculation. Many see being inferior to a woman as a major form of emasculation. They fear ambitious or powerful women. They lash out at women who seek high elected office. When elected, women are held to a higher standard than men are. Some women around the world have successfully achieved and held high office. Germany's chancellor, Angela Merkel, is one. Others have been less successful. In 2013, Julia Gillard was removed as Australian prime minister after only three years. Two female presidents—Dilma Rousseff of Brazil in 2016 and Park Geun-hye of South Korea in 2017—were impeached for corruption. Beinart notes that Rousseff was impeached "even though her male predecessors and some of her key male tormentors had likely done worse."

Park Geun-hye was the first woman elected president of South Korea. But in 2017, she was impeached for corruption.

Sady Doyle, writing in *Elle* magazine, thinks people must recognize sexism in politics. She says, "…sexism is still seen mostly as a matter of personality, not politics, even as sexism continues to operate with the power of a political force that can change the world." In a Huffington

Post article, two violence prevention experts expressed fears that Trump's presidency will increase violence against women. Rita Smith fears Trump's election has empowered men to treat women badly. "Even just the election itself had an impact on how men treated and talked about women," Smith said. Jackson Katz said, "We elected a man who is openly misogynistic, who has a decades-long public life of ridiculing, belittling and sexually objectifying women. The fact that we have lifted him up to be the president makes a powerful statement about our society and what we accept."

Most of the anger resulting from Trump's win came from Democrats or political liberals. But Susan Chira wrote a *New York Times* article titled "Since When Is Being a Woman a Liberal Cause?" She pointed out that many conservative women are also concerned about women's issues. Many do not favor Donald Trump. Of female Trump voters, 78 percent disliked his treatment of women. But they have conservative views on issues such as abortion, contraception, immigration, and criminal justice. Chira quotes Kori Schake, a research fellow at the conservative Hoover Institution: "It seems to me a better broader argument to make against the president is to join forces across gender lines, across all manner of lines, and argue for the respect of human dignity."

FIGHTING SEXISM FOR THE FUTURE

The United States has made great progress in women's rights during the last century. But the World Economic

Forum in 2015 still ranked the United States only twenty-eighth of 145 countries studied. It ranked seventy-ninth in percentage of women holding congressional seats. Whether at home, school, work, or in politics and the wider world, women will face sexism. How can teens combat it?

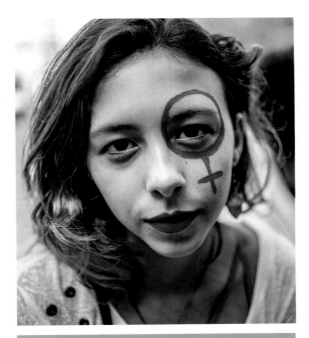

A young woman protests gender violence in Argentina in 2016. Horrific violence against women there has led to protests.

Children—both boys and girls—must learn equality from the beginning. They absorb information from people around them and from the media. Right now, they are not all learning equality. In a YouTube video on the Jimmy Kimmel channel, kids aged six to twelve were asked why men make more money than women. Many of the children responded, "Girls don't work as hard as the boys." Parents, teachers, and older siblings need to talk to young children about gender roles. They need to answer questions and make sure kids understand equality. This includes modeling equal treatment.

Girls can learn to recognize sexism in their own lives. Girls can stand up to obvious sexist behavior, such as sexist insults and inappropriate touching. They can call out the person doing it or report the behavior to adults. If adults dismiss the problem, girls can object. They can talk about unequal treatment. They can explain that such treatment is demeaning and hurtful. With practice, they can learn to stand up for themselves.

If little girls prefer building toys instead of dolls, they can ask for them. They can protest when boys get more help in school. If older girls want help with science or technology projects, they can ask for it. They can protest unequal treatment in all areas of life. Sometimes boys are not aware they are being sexist or hurtful. Just pointing it out can help. If they are doing it on purpose, they should learn it is not acceptable.

When girls learn to stand up for themselves, they are preparing for the challenges of adulthood. Gwendolyn Kansen, in Thought Catalog, discusses ways adult women can continue to stand up for their own equality. First, she says, women can think for themselves. They can base their self-worth on factors other than appearance. All women should learn more about science and politics. These topics are vital in modern society, and any intelligent woman should be able to discuss them. Every woman can become well-informed, develop her talents, and become a force for good in her community. She should be herself and not try to get ahead by being more like a man.

Because sexism exists, girls and women may have to work harder to reach their goals. But learning to identify and confront sexism this will help them build confidence and self-esteem. Every time a girl confronts sexism, she is making tomorrow's women stronger.

10 GREAT QUESTIONS TO ASK A SEXISM EXPERT

1. Is demeaning language to and about women harmful, and if so, why?
2. Does political correctness limit free speech, or is it necessary in a free, equal society?
3. What is a feminist, and who is included in the term?
4. Why is benevolent sexism hard to recognize and combat? What can be done about it?
5. Why do the rights of American women lag behind those of women in many other countries?
6. How does treating boys and girls differently during childhood promote sexism?
7. How are women and society affected by unequal treatment of girls in education?
8. How can teenage girls prepare to confront sexism they might face in the workplace?
9. How should girls and women respond to sexism in their homes and families?
10. How can girls and women best confront sexism in politics and society?

bias Prejudice for or against a certain person or group, in a way that leads to unfair treatment.

chief executive officer (CEO) The leader or highest-ranking officer in a company or corporation, responsible for making all major decisions for the company.

discrimination Unfair or biased treatment of a group, which often results in harm to that group or its individuals; for example, discrimination against women.

emasculation Weakening a man or stripping him of his "manhood" by depriving him of his male role or identity.

empower To give someone the power or authority to do something.

feminism The belief that men and women should be treated equally and should have equal rights and opportunities. People who believe in feminism are called feminists.

gender The state of being a man or a woman; the term "gender" is usually used when talking about social or cultural issues, while the term "sex" relates more to biology.

homophobic Having or showing dislike, hatred, fear, or prejudice against homosexuals.

househusband A man who stays home and takes care of the house and family while his wife earns the family income; also called stay-at-home parent (SAHP).

inauguration The ceremony that formally installs a new president into office.

institutional sexism Sexism that is ingrained into people in a society and is passed down, often thoughtlessly or unconsciously, from generation to generation.

LGBTQ+ Acronym referring to people who identify as lesbian, gay, bisexual, transgender, queer or questioning, and more. Other letters may be added to be more inclusive of nontraditional gender identification (LGBTQIA adds intersex and asexual).

misogyny Hatred, dislike, or contempt for women and girls; ingrained prejudice against women and girls.

political correctness Avoiding the use of certain words or phrases that might offend or insult certain people or groups, such as women or people of other races or ethnic groups.

precarious manhood The idea that manhood is a characteristic that must be earned and can be lost; many men greatly fear loss of manhood (emasculation).

prejudice A biased opinion or judgment against a group without cause or evidence; for example, prejudice against women.

sexism The unfair and biased treatment of women.

sexual harassment Uninvited and unwelcome sexual advances, by words or actions, that make the targeted person feel uncomfortable or endangered.

stereotype A widely held but oversimplified image or label of a group, such as women. For example, women are often stereotyped as weaker and less capable than men.

WAHP Work-at-home parent; a parent who works and conducts business from home, enabling a more flexible schedule and more time with children. One or both parents may be WAHPs.

American Association of University Women (AAUW)
1310 L Street NW, Suite 1000
Washington, DC 20005
(800) 326-2289
Website: http://www.aauw.org
Facebook: @AAUW.National
Twitter: @AAUW
Instagram: @aauwnational
The AAUW promotes equity and education for women
    and girls. For over one hundred years, they have
    taken positions on the issues of the day. Their latest
    campaign, Stand Up to Sexism, raises awareness of
    a culture that devalues women's work and contrib-
    utes to gender inequality.

Association of Women's Rights in Development (AWID)
215 Spadina Avenue, Suite 150
Toronto, ON M5T 2C7
Canada
(416) 594-3773
Website: https://www.awid.org
Facebook: @AWIDWomensRights
Twitter: @AWID
Instagram: @awidwomensrights
AWID is an international feminist organization com-
    mitted to achieving gender equality, sustainable
    development, and women's rights around the world.

League of Women Voters (LWV)
1730 M Street NW, Suite 1000
Washington, DC 20036-4508
(202) 429-1965
Website: http://lwv.org
Facebook: @leagueofwomenvoters
Twitter: @LWV
Instagram: @leagueofwomenvoters
The LWV works to improve government and engage
    all citizens in decisions that impact their lives. They
    work to expand voter participation, giving a voice to
    all Americans.

National Council of Women of Canada (NCWC)
PO Box 67099
Ottawa, ON K2A 4E4
Canada
(902) 422-8485
Website: http://www.ncwcanada.com
Facebook: @ncwcanada
Twitter: @ncwcanada
This nonprofit is a group of voluntary women's orga-
    nizations. They work together for women, families,
    and society.

National Organization for Women (NOW)
1100 H Street NW, Suite 300
Washington, DC 20005
(202) 628-8669
Website: http://now.org
Facebook: @NationalNOW

Twitter: @nationalNOW

NOW is the largest feminist organization in the United States. It takes a multi-issue and multistrategy approach to gender equality issues. One goal is the passage of an amendment to the US Constitution ensuring economic equality and equal rights for women.

Planned Parenthood Federation of America (PP)
123 William Street, 10th Floor
New York, NY 10038
(800) 230-PLAN or (800) 230-7526
Website: https://www.plannedparenthood.org
Facebook: @PlannedParenthood
Twitter: @PPFA
Instagram: @plannedparenthood

Planned Parenthood has served for one hundred years as an organization working for women's health care, education, and activism.

WEBSITES

Because of the changing nature of internet links, Rosen Publishing has developed an online list of websites related to the subject of this book. This site is updated regularly. Please use this link to access the list:

http://www.rosenlinks.com/NTKL/Sexism

Berlatsky, Noah. *Gendercide.* Farmington Hills, MI: Greenhaven Publishing, 2014.

Bickerstaff, Linda. *Violence Against Women: Public Health and Human Rights.* New York, NY: Rosen Publishing, 2010.

Cunningham, Anne. *Women Political Leaders.* New York, NY: Enslow Publishing, 2017.

Freedman, Jeri. *Women in the Workplace: Wages, Respect, and Equal Rights.* New York, NY: Rosen Publishing, 2010.

Furstinger, Nancy. *Women and Leadership.* New York, NY: Rosen Publishing, 2013.

Gay, Kathlyn. *Women Entrepreneurs.* New York, NY: Enslow Publishing, 2017.

Hanson-Harding, Alexandra. *Activism: Taking on Women's Issues.* New York, NY: Rosen Publishing, 2012.

Higgins, Nadia Abushanab. *Feminism: Reinventing the F-word.* Twenty-First Century Books, Amazon Digital Services, LLC, 2016.

Johanson, Paula. *Women Writers.* New York, NY: Enslow Publishing, 2017.

Kamberg, Mary-Lane. *Women: Body Image and Self-Esteem.* New York, NY: Rosen Publishing, 2012.

LaBella, Laura. *Women and Sports.* New York, NY: Rosen Publishing, 2012.

Mills, J. Elizabeth. *Expectations for Women: Confronting Stereotypes.* New York, NY: Rosen Publishing, 2012.

Niver, Heather Moore. *Women and Networking: Leveraging the Sisterhood.* New York, NY: Rosen Publishing, 2012.

Bennett, Jessica. *Feminist Fight Club: An Office Survival Manual for a Sexist Workplace.* New York, NY: Harper Wave, 2016.

Bomey, Nathan. "Sexism in the workplace is worse than you thought." *USA Today*, September 27, 2016. http://www.usatoday.com/story/money/2016/09/27/lean-in-study-women-in-the-workplace/91157026.

Bush, Mia. "US Women Make Strides Toward Equality, But Work Remains." VoaNews.com, March 8, 2016. http://www.voanews.com/a/international-womens-day-us-women-gender-equality-work-remains/3223162.html.

Harvard Business Review. "Women in the Workplace: A Research Roundup." September 2013 issue. https://hbr.org/2013/09/women-in-the-workplace-a-research-roundup.

International Labour Organization. "Gender Inequality and Women in the US Labor Force." Retrieved January 29, 2017. http://www.ilo.org/washington/areas/gender-equality-in-the-workplace/WCMS_159496/lang--en/index.htm.

Kaffer, Nancy. "Sexism Begins in the Toy Aisle." Daily Beast, November 29, 2014. http://www.thedailybeast.com/articles/2014/11/29/the-innate-sexism-of-christmas-toys.html.

Kansen, Gwendolyn. "18 Simple, Uncontroversial Ways Women Can Fight Sexism." ThoughtCatalog.com, May 21, 2015. http://thoughtcatalog.com

/gwendolyn-kansen/2015/05/18-simple
-uncontroversial-ways-women-can-fight-sexism.

Leaper, Campbell, and Christina Spears Brown.
"Sexism in Schools." *Advances in child development and behavior* 47:189-223, Oct. 2014. https://
www.researchgate.net/publication/267730537
_Sexism_in_Schools.

Leygerman, Dina. "You Are Not Equal. I'm Sorry."
Medium.com, January 22, 2017.
https://medium.com/@dinachka82/about-your-poem
-1f26a7585a6f#.invakglsg.

Ruiz, Michelle. "What Sexual Harassment at Work
Really Looks Like." *Cosmopolitan*, February 16,
2015. http://www.cosmopolitan.com/career/a36462
/sexual-harassment-at-work.

Schank, Hana, and Elizabeth Wallace. "The Sexism
They Faced." *The Atlantic*, December 19, 2016.
https://www.theatlantic.com/business
/archive/2016/12/sexism/509213.

Schuller, Tom. *The Paula Principle. How and why
women work below their level of competence.*
Melbourne, Australia: Scribe Publications, 2017.

Tannenbaum, Melanie. "The Problem When Sexism Just
Sounds So Darn Friendly…" *Scientific American,*
April 2, 2013. https://blogs.scientificamerican.com
/psysociety/benevolent-sexism.

Valcour, Monique. "Navigating Tradeoffs in a Dual-Career
Marriage." *Harvard Business Review*, April 14, 2015.
https://hbr.org/2015/04/navigating-tradeoffs-in-a
-dual-career-marriage.

ABOUT THE AUTHOR

Carol Hand has a PhD in zoology with a specialization in ecology and environmental problems. She has taught at the college level, worked for standardized testing companies, developed multimedia science and technology curricula, and written more than forty science and technology books for young people. Having both university and workplace experience, she has first-hand experience dealing with the challenges women face at school and work.

PHOTO CREDITS